Francis Frith's

Wokingham
and Bracknell

Photographic Memories

Francis Frith's
Wokingham
and Bracknell

Trevor Ottlewski

First published in the United Kingdom in 2001 by
Frith Book Company Ltd

Paperback Edition 2001
ISBN 1-85937-329-1

Reprinted in Paperback 2004
ISBN 1-85837-329-1

British Library Cataloguing in Publication Data

Francis Frith's Wokingham & Bracknell
Trevor Ottlewski

Frith Book Company Ltd
Frith's Barn, Teffont,
Salisbury, Wiltshire SP3 5QP
Tel: +44 (0) 1722 716 376
Email: info@francisfrith.co.uk
www.francisfrith.co.uk

Printed and bound in Great Britain

Front Cover: Wokingham, Town Hall c1955 W123044

The colour-tinting is for illustrative purposes only, and is not intended to be historically accurate

Contents

Francis Frith: Victorian Pioneer   7

Frith's Archive - A Unique Legacy   10

Wokingham and Bracknell - An Introduction   12

Wokingham and the Nine Mile Ride   16

Bracknell and Neighbouring Parishes   44

Around Ascot   60

Crowthorne Village   66

Finchampstead and Eversley   76

Index   87

Free Mounted Print Voucher   91

Francis Frith: *Victorian Pioneer*

FRANCIS FRITH, Victorian founder of the world-famous photographic archive, was a complex and multi-talented man. A devout Quaker and a highly successful Victorian businessman, he was both philosophical by nature and pioneering in outlook.

By 1855 Francis Frith had already established a wholesale grocery business in Liverpool, and sold it for the astonishing sum of £200,000, which is the equivalent today of over £15,000,000. Now a very rich man, he was able to indulge his passion for travel. As a child he had pored over travel books written by early explorers, and his fancy and imagination had been stirred by family holidays to the sublime mountain regions of Wales and Scotland. 'What lands of spirit-stirring and enriching scenes and places!' he had written. He was to return to these scenes of grandeur in later years to 'recapture the thousands of vivid and tender memories', but with a different purpose. Now in his thirties, and captivated by the new science of photography, Frith set out on a series of pioneering journeys to the Nile regions that occupied him from 1856 until 1860.

Intrigue and Adventure

He took with him on his travels a specially-designed wicker carriage that acted as both dark-room and sleeping chamber. These far-flung journeys were packed with intrigue and adventure. In his life story, written when he was sixty-three, Frith tells of being held captive by bandits, and of fighting 'an awful midnight battle to the very point of surrender with a deadly pack of hungry, wild dogs'. Sporting flowing Arab costume, Frith arrived at Akaba by camel sixty years before Lawrence, where he encountered 'desert princes and rival sheikhs, blazing with jewel-hilted swords'.

During these extraordinary adventures he was assiduously exploring the desert regions bordering the Nile and patiently recording the antiquities and peoples with his camera. He was the first photographer to venture beyond the sixth cataract. Africa was still the mysterious 'Dark Continent', and Stanley and Livingstone's historic meeting was a decade into the future. The conditions for picture taking confound belief. He laboured for hours in his wicker dark-room in the sweltering heat of the desert, while the volatile chemicals fizzed dangerously in their trays. Often he was forced to work in remote tombs and caves where conditions were cooler. Back in London he exhibited his photographs and was 'rapturously cheered' by members of the Royal Society. His reputation as a photographer was made overnight. An eminent modern historian has likened their impact on the population of the time to that on our own generation of the first photographs taken on the surface of the moon.

Venture of a Life-Time

Characteristically, Frith quickly spotted the opportunity to create a new business as a specialist publisher of photographs. He lived in an era of immense and sometimes violent change. For the poor in the early part of Victoria's reign work was a drudge and the hours long, and people had precious little free time to enjoy themselves. Most had no transport other than a cart or gig at their disposal, and had not travelled far beyond the boundaries of their own town or village. However,

by the 1870s, the railways had threaded their way across the country, and Bank Holidays and half-day Saturdays had been made obligatory by Act of Parliament. All of a sudden the ordinary working man and his family were able to enjoy days out and see a little more of the world.

With characteristic business acumen, Francis Frith foresaw that these new tourists would enjoy having souvenirs to commemorate their days out. In 1860 he married Mary Ann Rosling and set out with the intention of photographing every city, town and village in Britain. For the next thirty years he travelled the country by train and by pony and trap, producing fine photographs of seaside resorts and beauty spots that were keenly bought by millions of Victorians. These prints were painstakingly pasted into family albums and pored over during the dark nights of winter, rekindling precious memories of summer excursions.

The Rise of Frith & Co

Frith's studio was soon supplying retail shops all over the country. To meet the demand he gathered about him a small team of photographers, and published the work of independent artist-photographers of the calibre of Roger Fenton and Francis Bedford. In order to gain some understanding of the scale of Frith's business one only has to look at the catalogue issued by Frith & Co in 1886: it runs to some 670 pages, listing not only many thousands of views of the British Isles but also many photographs of most European countries, and China, Japan, the USA and Canada — note the sample page shown on page 9 from the hand-written *Frith & Co* ledgers detailing pictures taken. By 1890 Frith had created the greatest specialist photographic publishing company in the

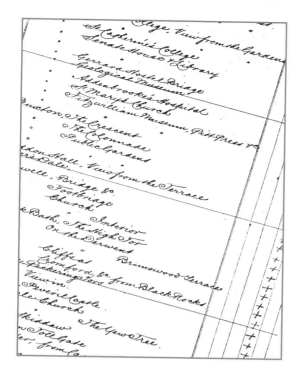

Frith's death, a new card measuring 5.5 x 3.5 inches became the standard format, but it was not until 1902 that the divided back came into being, with address and message on one face and a full-size illustration on the other. *Frith & Co* were in the vanguard of postcard development, and Frith's sons Eustace and Cyril continued their father's monumental task, expanding the number of views offered to the public and recording more and more places in Britain, as the coasts and countryside were opened up to mass travel.

Francis Frith died in 1898 at his villa in Cannes, his great project still growing. The archive he created continued in business for another seventy years. By 1970 it contained over a third of a million pictures of 7,000 cities, towns and villages. The massive photographic record Frith has left to us stands as a living monument to a special and very remarkable man.

world, with over 2,000 outlets – more than the combined number that Boots and WH Smith have today! The picture on the right shows the *Frith & Co* display board at Ingleton in the Yorkshire Dales (left of window). Beautifully constructed with a mahogany frame and gilt inserts, it could display up to a dozen local scenes.

Postcard Bonanza

The ever-popular holiday postcard we know today took many years to develop. In 1870 the Post Office issued the first plain cards, with a pre-printed stamp on one face. In 1894 they allowed other publishers' cards to be sent through the mail with an attached adhesive halfpenny stamp. Demand grew rapidly, and in 1895 a new size of postcard was permitted called the court card, but there was little room for illustration. In 1899, a year after

Frith's Archive: *A Unique Legacy*

FRANCIS FRITH'S legacy to us today is of immense significance and value, for the magnificent archive of evocative photographs he created provides a unique record of change in 7,000 cities, towns and villages throughout Britain over a century and more. Frith and his fellow studio photographers revisited locations many times down the years to update their views, compiling for us an enthralling and colourful pageant of British life and character.

We tend to think of Frith's sepia views of Britain as nostalgic, for most of us use them to conjure up memories of places in our own lives with which we have family associations. It often makes us forget that to Francis Frith they were records of daily life as it was actually being lived in the cities, towns and villages of his day. The Victorian age was one of great and often bewildering change for ordinary people, and though the pictures evoke an impression of slower times, life was as busy and hectic as it is today.

We are fortunate that Frith was a photographer of the people, dedicated to recording the minutiae of everyday life. For it is this sheer wealth of visual data, the painstaking chronicle of changes in dress, transport, street layouts, buildings, housing, engineering and landscape that captivates us so much today. His remarkable images offer us a powerful link with the past and with the lives of our ancestors.

Today's Technology

Computers have now made it possible for Frith's many thousands of images to be accessed almost instantly. In the Frith archive today, each photograph is carefully 'digitised' then stored on a CD Rom. Frith archivists can locate a single photograph amongst thousands within seconds. Views can be catalogued and sorted under a variety of categories of place and content to the immediate benefit of researchers.

Inexpensive reference prints can be created for them at the touch of a mouse button, and a wide range of books and other printed materials assembled and published for a wider, more general readership. The day-to-day workings of the archive are very different from how they were in Francis Frith's time: imagine the herculean task of sorting through eleven tons of glass negatives as Frith had to do to locate a particular sequence of pictures! Yet the archive still prides itself on maintaining the same high standards of excellence laid down by

See Frith at www.francisfrith.co.uk

Francis Frith, including the painstaking cataloguing and indexing of every view.

It is curious to reflect on how the internet now allows researchers in America and elsewhere greater instant access to the archive than Frith himself ever enjoyed. Many thousands of individual views can be called up on screen within seconds on one of the Frith internet sites, enabling people living continents away to revisit the streets of their ancestral home town, or view places in Britain where they have enjoyed holidays. Many overseas researchers welcome the chance to view special theme selections, such as transport, sports, costume and ancient monuments.

We are certain that Francis Frith would have heartily approved of these modern developments in imaging techniques, for he himself was always working at the very limits of Victorian photographic technology.

The Value of the Archive Today

Because of the benefits brought by the computer, Frith's images are increasingly studied by social historians, by researchers into genealogy and ancestory, by architects, town planners, and by teachers and schoolchildren involved in local history projects.

In addition, the archive offers every one of us an opportunity to examine the places where we and our families have lived and worked down the years. Highly successful in Frith's own era, the archive is now, a century and more on, entering a new phase of popularity.

The Past in Tune with the Future

Historians consider the Francis Frith Collection to be of prime national importance. It is the only archive of its kind remaining in private ownership and has been valued at a million pounds. However, this figure is now rapidly increasing as digital technology enables more and more people around the world to enjoy its benefits.

Francis Frith's archive is now housed in an historic timber barn in the beautiful village of Teffont in Wiltshire. Its founder would not recognize the archive office as it is today. In place of the many thousands of dusty boxes containing glass plate negatives and an all-pervading odour of photographic chemicals, there are now ranks of computer screens. He would be amazed to watch his images travelling round the world at unimaginable speeds through network and internet lines.

The archive's future is both bright and exciting. Francis Frith, with his unshakeable belief in making photographs available to the greatest number of people, would undoubtedly approve of what is being done today with his lifetime's work. His photographs, depicting our shared past, are now bringing pleasure and enlightenment to millions around the world a century and more after his death.

Wokingham & Bracknell
An Introduction

WOKINGHAM AND BRACKNELL were for centuries within the bounds of Windsor Forest, which was a mixture of woodland, heathland and fields, together with other natural features. Strict forest laws were applied to its inhabitants that must also have influenced the way in which the area was allowed to develop. It served as a royal hunting ground and a valuable source of timber, so care for both was considered of paramount importance.

The Civil War brought about a period of neglect, following which efforts were made for improvement. During the 18th century further problems arose, including an increase in crime, notably the exploits of a gang known as the 'Wokingham Blacks', so called because they blackened their faces. They were eventually captured, following which a number were tried and hanged. Suffering a gradual decline, the forest survived until the Enclosure Act of 1813, when a decision was made to keep and care for a core area, but give up rights over the remainder. Pine plantations replaced some of the former heath land, and the availability of large expanses of land heralded changes in use that have continued to the present day. It was against this background that the towns of Wokingham and Bracknell developed, in quite contrasting ways despite their close proximity.

Wokingham's location is recorded on a

milestone in the town centre as being seven miles to Reading and 32 miles to London. No prehistoric settlement has been found; a few isolated finds of stone age tools would tend to suggest it was visited, rather than settled on. There was a small amount of Romano-British activity outside the town, perhaps of an industrial nature; elsewhere at least two hoards of Roman coins have been found, but as yet Roman activity is not considered to have been especially significant.

The name 'Wokingham' is of Saxon origin and suggests a tribal homestead. Early records note the existence of a chapel that was dedicated to All Saints in the late 12th century. As a town, Wokingham really became established with the granting of a market charter to the Bishop of Salisbury in 1219. Market towns were few and, serving a wide area, it must have attracted traders who wished to settle close to their place of business. In time, rights were granted to hold fairs on specified days of the year, providing an additional draw and enhancing Wokingham's position as a place of trade. Today a significant number of buildings survive from the 15th century and their quality suggests a well-established town, providing a relatively prosperous way of life for some.

Industry is known to have existed from the 14th century, notably bell founding. Wokingham bells were supplied across a number of counties; a bell predating 1383 still survives in Dorchester Abbey, Dorchester on Thames, Oxfordshire. Under different owners, their manufacture continued in the town until moving elsewhere in the early 17th century. Wokingham remained a reasonably prosperous place until the 1640s, when events of the Civil War almost brought the town to its knees. Although not a battleground, the town suffered from the demands of both Cavaliers and Roundheads for food and supplies. When provisions were all but exhausted and demand could no longer be met, punishment was delivered by the burning of a number of buildings and it is thought to have been some years before the town fully recovered.

Over the years a variety of different charities have been founded for the benefit of Wokingham residents, a number of which originated in the 17th century. Perhaps best known is that founded by Henry Lucas, who, in 1663, left money to build and maintain an almshouse for 16 deserving men and a master. They could be selected from any of the specified parishes, which totalled about 32, including that of Wokingham. A fine brick building was constructed, incorporating a chapel, and in addition, outhouses, a brew house, and a walled garden. The Drapers Company became trustees, and for just over 330 years residents enjoyed the tranquil setting of the almshouse. This link ended in 2001 when Lucas Hospital was sold by the trustees and the proceeds used to continue the charity elsewhere. The building, however, remains in all its glory as Wokingham's only grade one listed residence. Another charity, founded in 1661 by George Staverton, became something of a notorious event. He gave instructions for the purchase of a bull, the meat of which was to be given to the poor; the sale of its offal and hide was to provide further benefits. The deed took place annually on 21 December, St Thomas's day, in the market place, where the bull was baited, supposedly to improve the meat, prior to slaughter. Large crowds gathered to watch the event at which trained dogs attempted to 'pin' the bull, and if considered worthy were awarded a prize. It seems the event was used by some as an excuse for rowdy behaviour, and although popular with many, was finally banned by the Corporation in 1821, after which the bull was merely paraded prior to its slaughter.

During the 18th century, although new houses

were built, many of the existing timber-framed houses were modernised by the addition of a brick façade with sash windows and panelled doors. As a rural town, agriculture remained an important occupation. Throughout the 18th century, many of the existing businesses continued, including those of wool sorting and the silk industry (for which Wokingham is often considered notable). Tanning was also an important business; with access to running water, a market and the local availability of oak bark, the area was an ideal location to carry out the process.

The Windsor Forest Turnpike was established in 1759. The improvements in the quality of the road surface which followed led to a regular coach service, which, in time, extended all the way to London, making a return journey achievable in a single day.

The 19th century saw great development. The coming of the railway, as in most other places, allowed the movement of goods and people to a distance and at a pace never previously possible. 1849 saw the opening of the line from Reading to Guildford and in 1859 a further line gave direct access to London. In the 1850s the new Union Workhouse was built in Barkham Road. A new town hall was built to replace the earlier timber-framed hall and was opened in 1860. Churches were built by the Baptists, Primitive Methodists, Wesleyan Methodists, in addition to the church of St Paul

which required a second parish to be formed within the town. Wokingham enjoyed the patronage of the Walter family, owners of the huge Bearwood Estate and founders, proprietors and printers of 'The Times' newspaper, whose generosity provided a number of new buildings for the benefit of Wokingham people, including St Paul's church and its rectory. New schools were built and the town began expanding into areas that had hitherto been fields.

Much of Wokingham's traditional nature survived into the 1950s. It was really during the 1960s and 1970s the town centre suffered, as did many others, from the development of shops and offices of insensitive design to their surroundings, and during which many old and interesting buildings were demolished.

Bracknell lies a few miles from Wokingham but, unlike its neighbour, for centuries remained a small forest settlement. It must have benefited from its roadside position and gained some trade from passing travellers. On Norden's 1607 map of Windsor Forest, two small and separate settlements are shown, and although in close proximity, use an earlier spelling to show, Old Brecknoll and New Brecknoll.

The Windsor Forest Turnpike of 1759 changed the forest track to a main road; New Bracknell was now in a position to develop as a place of trade. Coaches to and from London stopped regularly, and

the area attracted a number of new wealthy residents. One of the more unusual ways to cash in on the traveller was reputedly undertaken by the landlord of the Hinds Head. Obviously a villain of the highest order, having provided beds for moneyed and weary travellers, the story goes, he murdered them in the night and robbed them of their belongings.

The Enclosure Act of 1813 would have freed much of the area from Crown control and allowed owners to develop their land in different ways. The environment must still have appeared rather forbidding as, in 1822, the journalist William Cobbett described the land between Oakingham and Sunninghill "as bleak, as barren, and as villainous heath, as ever man set his eyes on". In 1849 it was proposed that Bracknell, with a population of 500, required a church. The decision was made to build Holy Trinity Church, and a new parish of Bracknell was created. The railway came in 1856, improving access to Bracknell still further. During the 19th century, a large and successful market existed and the area around Bracknell became noted for the manufacture of bricks and tiles. By the late 1880s, high street shops included the very large store of Thomas Lawrence who also owned a number of brickyards.

The 20th century was to bring Bracknell's most dramatic change. The New Towns Act of 1946 was designed to resolve the problem of the acute housing shortage following the war. In 1948, Bracknell was chosen as one of the new towns. In 1949 the Bracknell Development Corporation was established - with much local opposition to their proposals. The vision was to create a self-contained country town, with town amenities and country benefits, with workplaces, shops, and schools within easy reach, and most of the new residents drawn from Greater London. The first houses in Priestwood were occupied in 1951 and building has continued ever since, with most of the old Bracknell swept away. There are now areas of the new town that are being redeveloped and the original planned population of 25,000 has more than doubled.

Today the town boasts a theatre, arts centre, hotels, a variety of sports facilities, and has proved attractive as a location to many multinational companies, particularly those of a hi-tech nature. New residents are still arriving, houses are still being built, and Bracknell continues to grow.

Both Wokingham and Bracknell have developed in different ways, as have the villages around them. Some have altered less than others, but all have changed, and by looking at old photographs we can see the differences that have taken place, which for some will bring back memories and for others portray a period they never knew. But for all, they remain a valuable record of our past.

Wokingham
and the Nine Mile Ride

Wokingham
All Saints Church 1906 57029
A chapel is known to have existed from the late 12th century when it was dedicated to All Saints, although little information has survived to provide us with any detail. The present church is believed to date from the 14th century, but has undergone numerous additions and alterations, which include a major restoration in the mid-19th century, much of it under the care of the architect Henry Woodyer. The tower is built in a local conglomerate material known as pudding stone, and inside the church a number of the columns are chalk.

Wokingham, All Saints Church c1955 W123015
Viewed from Peach Street, the Ship Inn is on the left, with the sign of Simonds Brewery hanging on a bracket, not - as it may first appear - attached to the church. Little has changed regarding the church except for the addition of a war memorial, the cross of which is visible in the centre of the picture.

Wokingham, Rose Street c1955 W123014
The 15th-century building in the foreground has had a variety of uses, including that of a public house named The Cricketers which ran from the mid 19th century until its closure in 1909. This picture shows it as a fish and chip shop. In recent years it has doubled as a tailor's workroom with private accommodation above. The tall narrow building immediately to the left was at one time home to James Seaward, who was reputedly the inspiration for the character of Tom in Charles Kingsley's book 'The Water Babies'. Beyond is a fine run of 15th- and 16th-century buildings.

**Wokingham
Rose Street 1906**
57028
In those days the young girl with her large wooden hoop could use the street as a playground with little fear from traffic. The timber-framed buildings behind her were eventually demolished. Today the site is occupied by new housing, with a re-routed exit for Cross Street, which in this photograph is shown emerging near the gas lamp.

◄ **Wokingham Town Hall 1906** 57025
Opened in June 1860, the Town Hall cost £3,505 to build, and provided space for the County Police Station, with cells and an exercise yard, a courtroom and council offices. By this date, the Fire Brigade were also housed here and operated a steam powered fire engine.

◄ Wokingham
Peach Street c1955

W123020

The popularity of shopping by bicycle is evident, as was the confidence that your means of transport would still be there on your return. This scene is buzzing with shoppers, and among those enjoying their patronage were Bailey's Delicatessen, Farmer's greengrocers, Bata the shoe shop, Sanders Brothers, and Woolworths.

▼ Wokingham
Ye Olde Rose Inne c1965

W123111

The Rose originally occupied a building on the north east side of Market Place, but moved to this site in 1844. Walkers store is shown on the right, whilst to the left we can see an attractive building occupied by Barclays Bank, now sadly demolished. In its place stands a rather lacklustre replacement.

◄ Wokingham, Town Hall 1906

57026a

The entrance to Peach Street can just be seen on the far right, as can the hanging sign of The Rose Hotel. The Red Lion Inn has a large gas lamp attached to the front wall on which its name is written. Next door is the business of Mr Carter, boot and shoemaker, whose shop front remains virtually unaltered to this day, but now serves the business of Wellingtons the jewellers. It is hard to imagine this scene today when confronted by the market stalls, traffic lights, bollards and paving that have been added over the years.

◄ **Wokingham
Denmark Street
c1955** W123029
Beyond the lamp post
we can just see the
entrance to the Drill Hall,
constructed in 1881 and
one of the properties
built through the
generosity of John Walter
III. Across the road a
gentleman is standing in
one of the doorways of
what were known as the
Exchange Cottages.

◄ Wokingham Town Hall from Market Place c1955

W123017

This street scene is much altered from that of the 1906 photograph. Cars in the market place, road signs to direct the traffic and the addition of electric street lighting are just a few of the changes. However, on the right we can see the sign of Sale's, the seed merchants, who still occupied premises to the left of The Red Lion.

▼ Wokingham Denmark Street c1955

W123016

In this picture the timber-framed Exchange Cottages are on the left and a car is parked outside the Royal Exchange public house. Partially obscured on the right is the sign of Trills cycle shop, and a little further along the business of E Gosling, purveyor of meat, fish, game, and poultry.

◄ Wokingham Town Hall c1955

W123044

Hussey & Son were ironmongers who had been operating from the same shop for many years, next door to which was Boots chemist, who also advertised themselves as having a Boots Booklovers Library. Looking to the far side of Market Place we see the coal office of Talbot & Son.

**Wokingham
Broad Street 1906**
57024
Rednall's dispensing chemist and druggist occupied the premises on the corner of Market Place and Broad Street. Directly opposite was Maris, the saddler and harness maker, beyond which a black and white bollard marked the entrance to a (then much narrower) Rose Street.

Wokingham, Town Hall c1955 W123018
Timothy Whites occupied the corner premises, continuing the tradition of its use as a chemists' shop. Today the building remains but is now a bank and offices. The decorative shop front and blocked windows above are still a recognisable feature.

Wokingham, Broad Street c1955 W123031

The shop on the left provided not only a hairdressing service but at least three different brands of cigarette. On the right, we can see the Westminster bank, and next door the estate agents Martin & Pole, the upper floor of which bears the name of the Leek and Morlands building society.

Wokingham, Broad Street c1960 W123105

In the early 17th century the long low building on the left was in use as the George Inn, but by 1960 was a café and cake shop. The large Victorian building on the opposite corner of Rose Street had various uses, but at this time was part of the Heelas of Wokingham department store.

Wokingham, Broad Street c1960 W123100

This photograph must have been taken on a sunny day as there are strong shadows and the shops have their awnings out. One shop front not in the shade was that of the Wokingham Laundry Co, pictured to the right of the cyclists.

Wokingham, Broad Street c1955 W123002

From this elevated view point we get the impression of what must have appeared a somewhat green street. Across the road large trees obscure the front of Montague House, whilst on this side, pollard trees mark the edge of the road and in the foreground a thick green hedge can be seen in front of The Elms.

Wokingham
Shoot End from Broad Street 1906 57026
At the junction of Broad Street and Shute End there was only a single gas lamp, where now are so many traffic lights and bollards. The ivy-clad Grosvenor School lies ahead with iron railings surrounding its frontage.

Wokingham
Broad Street 1906 57026c
The shop of Mr W H Howard had been mostly concerned with the supply of ironmongery, plumbing and gas fittings, although with the advent of motoring he clearly saw the opportunity for business as a car mechanic. However, it would appear he did not give up the former business, but ran both from the same premises.

Wokingham
Tudor House c1955 W123001
At some time after the Grosvenor School had moved, the rendering was removed from the building and 16th-century timber-framing revealed. A jetty was reinstated on the left, and windows more in keeping with its age were installed. This view of the building shows it with much the same appearance we see today.

Wokingham
Martin's Swimming Pool c1955 W123010
This pool was named after William Thomas Martin, a successful local businessman. He lived on The Terrace and in the early 1930s at the rear of his property he built an elaborate swimming pool surrounded by landscaped gardens, which he opened to the public. It was bought by the Borough Council after the war and remained in popular use for many years. In 1992 against much local opposition, it was sold for development and the proceeds put towards a new swimming pool.

Wokingham
Reading Road 1906 57027a
Looking along the unmade surface of Shute End, we can see St Paul's Parish Rooms and clock tower marking the start of Reading Road. Around the 1870s landscaping took place on the raised ground to the right, after which it was named The Terrace.

Wokingham
The Queen's Head 1906 57027c
There was no mistaking the service offered by this establishment on The Terrace. The building, which dates from the 15th century, is notable as the only building in Wokingham known to have a cruck frame as part of its construction.

Wokingham, The Terrace c1955 W123033
The Terrace Café, a popular place to meet for afternoon tea, offered an alternative place of refreshment to its neighbour, The Queen's Head. A little further along, the building with a long sloping roof, left of the telegraph pole, is reputedly the oldest in Wokingham with an internal timber frame believed to date from the mid 14th century, although it is well disguised with a later brick shell. Today a roundabout is in the foreground to assist the flow of traffic to and from Station Road.

Wokingham, Station Road c1955 W123034
The Hope and Anchor, seen here on the right, has changed little in the present day, but now includes the small gabled building on its left, which had been a blacksmiths for many years. Today the British Legion hall will be found to the rear of the next building along, which in this photograph bears the name 'Wokingham Ex-Servicemen's Club'.

Wokingham, Public Rest Gardens c1955 W123006
The building on the right, largely obscured by trees, was built c1869 as the rectory to St Paul's church. Bought by the Rural District Council in the late 1930s, it remains in council use to this day. Additional offices have been added to the old rectory, and together with a carpark, have absorbed most of the former garden.

Wokingham, Reading Road 1906 57027
Looking in the direction of the town, the Holt estate lay behind the trees on the left. Two large gas lamps flank the lych-gate to St Paul's church on the right. There appears to be a hard path across the road in line with the gate, presumably laid to protect pedestrians from the dust and mud of the road.

Wokingham, St Pauls Church c1955 W123095
This less familiar view of the church benefits from a lack of vegetative growth. The church exterior is rubble faced with dressed Bath stone and the windows have an interesting decorative style. The glazing includes a series in stained glass by Hardman, which illustrates the life of St Paul.

◄ **Wokingham Kingsmere Lake c1965**
W123103
Many older residents have fond memories of Kingsmere, that was particularly enticing on hot summer days. It became a popular private club that ran for a number of years before closing. Later, a falling water level and excessive weed caused concern, but today in the grounds of a private residence it is well maintained and a haven for wildlife.

▼ Wokingham, St Sebastian's Church, Nine Mile Ride 1910 62916
The church was built in 1864, mainly to cater for the religious well-being of local heath dwellers. The brick church was designed by the architect W Butterfield, but received some upgrading in the 1880s. In the foreground, Nine Mile Ride can be seen as an unmade road.

▼ Wokingham, St Sebastian's Church, Nine Mile Ride 1910 62917
A small but decorative wooden bell tower houses a single bell and is perched neatly on the gable end. A school was built nearby to provide for the educational needs of local children. Today both the church and school continue in popular use.

▲ Wokingham Nine Mile Ride Post Office 1909 61942
Close to the junction of Nine Mile Ride, New Wokingham Road and Honey Hill, we can see Chappell's Store, clearly the local retailer for Salmon's Teas but also providing the facility of a Post Office to the scattered local community. At this date, a dog could safely stand and wait in the road until the next traveller came into view.

◄ **Wokingham
Nine Mile Ride 1909**
61943
Looking in the opposite
direction to the photograph
61942, Chappell's Store is
on the right, but we see an
equally rural scene. Today,
we would see St Sebastian's
Memorial Hall on the left
and a roundabout at the
road junction in the
foreground.

Wokingham, The Lodge, London Open Air Sanitorium, Pinewood 1909 61944
This is the main Sanitorium entrance viewed from Nine Mile Ride. Today the entrance and lodge remain, although the drive is wider, leading to a modern building belonging to the computer company Hewlett Packard. Nine Mile Ride is now a busy main road.

Wokingham, London Open Air Sanitorium, Pinewood 1910 62912
The clean air and scent of the pines must have been welcomed by the London residents suffering from lung complaints, who were sent to Pinewood for their treatment. The verandahs and large open windows were all designed to provide the maximum opportunity for breathing fresh air.

Wokingham, Green Walk, London Open Air Sanitorium 1910 62915
This view shows the healthy practice of taking the air. The two gentlemen pictured are reclining on loungers in a setting of thick pine woodland, no doubt an important part of their treatment. It would appear that covered shelters allowed this activity to continue whatever the weather.

Bracknell
and Neighbouring Parishes

Warfield
Church 1901 46909
Parts of the present church of St Michael the Archangel date from 1087, although a chapel was recorded as being in Warfield from Saxon times. The church was enlarged considerably during the 14th and 15th centuries. G E Street, the architect, oversaw much of the 19th-century restoration. Bracknell parish was, to a large extent, carved out of the parish of Warfield.

Bracknell
Holy Trinity Church 1901 46898
Although apparently built in brick, the church has been faced in knapped flint, giving it
an earlier appearance than its mid-19th-century date might suggest. Today the church
stands on a small piece of land sandwiched between two roads.

**Bracknell
Church Road 1901**
46897
The tower of Holy
Trinity Church is visible
above the solidly-built
houses which line the
road. Many of the
frontages have low walls
above which stand
attractive iron railings.
The man with the
handcart was perhaps
making an early
morning delivery.

▼ **Bracknell, The Market Inn 1951** B172002
With the railway station just out of view to the left, this was the nearest hotel and inn for railway passengers. The cars are characteristic of the age, and a close look at the one on the left will reveal it as a three-wheeler. The inn is easily recognisable today but is now named 'The Goose'.

▼ **Bracknell, Old Manor Hotel c1955** B172010
On the left is the Old Manor Hotel - one of the few buildings to survive Bracknell's redevelopment. The white building on the right had been The Hinds Head, the landlord of which reputedly robbed and murdered guests in the 18th century. In the 19th century, a successful cattle market was founded at the rear of the inn.

▲ **Bracknell High Street 1901** 46896
Perhaps this is an early morning scene as shoppers are few, although a lady appears to have spotted something of interest in the shop window of Timothy & Sandwith the chemist. Horse-drawn carts can be seen waiting at the side of the road.

◀ **Bracknell
High Street c1960** B172048

On the right is Teetgens, a high-class grocer. Beyond is the Post Office, built in the early 1930s, and next door is Sirls. We can see the rear of a Morris Traveller as it drives down the middle of the street. To the left is Frisby's shoe store then Jacksons, with Smiths Coachbuilders in the foreground. Today, only the Post Office remains, new buildings having replaced the others. The street is now pedestrianised and running across the foreground is the elevated road called The Ring.

**Bracknell
High Street 1901**
46895
The store of Thomas Lawrence & Sons dominates the street scene. Nowadays it would be described as a department store. Their stock ranged from food and drink to outfitting and furnishings. The company is best remembered for their manufacture of bricks, as portrayed in their decorative brick façade.

◄ **Bracknell High Street 1901**
46894
In the foreground a young boy appears rather smart in his straw boater. He is looking across to the lady in black, who is standing beside a pram. Judging by the quantity of lines carried on the telegraph poles, it would appear that a number of telephones had been installed in the area.

◀ **Bracknell
High Street 1901** 46893
Towards the bottom of the
High Street, The Bull Inn
advertises good stabling
above the sign for the
'Weekly Dispatch'. Further
along is the shop of
Colebrook & Co,
butchers, who supplied a
variety of meat products
and had a number of
shops in the area.

▼ **Bracknell
High Street c1960** B172056
Looking up the High Street we
can see what changes had
taken place by the 1960s. The
road surface was tarmac and a
'Keep Left' bollard was
necessary to direct the traffic.
A number of new shops had
added to the range of goods
available, including Pinnel &
Mills, who sold materials for
home decorating and across
the road, Jim Sheehan the
motorcycle dealer. Roadside
parking was freely available.

◀ **Bracknell
The Horse and Groom
c1955** B172001
This public house
survives today as part of
a restaurant chain. The
building originated in the
17th century and is now
a grade II listed building.
Although it still retains
some of its rural setting,
the road in the
foreground is now a dual
carriageway and a main
route from Bracknell to
the M3 motorway.

◄ **Easthampstead Church c1960** E144008
From Reeds Hill this view towards the Crowthorne Road shows, on the left, buildings that were part of the Churchill House complex. On the right, White Cottage dating from the 17th century is now a listed building.

◀ **Bracknell
Priestwood Square
c1955** B172026
The neighbourhood of Priestwood was the first of Bracknell's New Town developments to be occupied. This must have been considered the latest in architectural fashion, built with the intention of providing a shopping area within easy reach of the local community.

▼ **Easthampstead
Church 1901** 46901
The church of St Michael and St Mary Magdalene had its origins in the 12th century. Due to its poor condition, it was replaced in the 1860s by the church we see today. Some of its earlier memorials and artefacts were re-housed in the new structure. It has some stained glass windows by the artist Edward Burne-Jones.

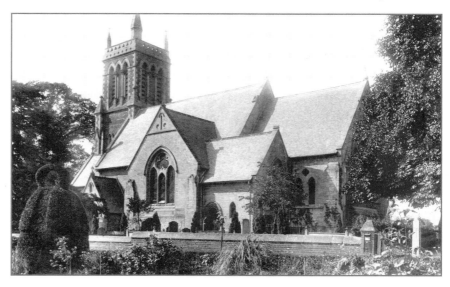

◀ **Easthampstead
Borough Green and
Foxhill Schools c1965**
E144010
The historic parish of Easthampstead, was to a considerable extent developed as part of Bracknell New Town. Borough Green and Foxhill schools were built to serve the local community, although Foxhill School was relocated to Pond Moor Road in the 1970s. Today the buildings continue in use as Brakenhale School.

Easthampstead, Point Royal c1965 E144018
Completed in February 1964, Point Royal was designed by the architectural practice of Arup Associates and was of much interest to avant-garde architects of the day. Much of its support is derived from a central core, in which a lift is contained, providing access to the 102 apartments. Its contribution to architectural history has been recognised. Now set within a conservation area, it is a grade II listed building.

Binfield, Church and Lychgate 1901 46905
Early parts of All Saints Church are built in a conglomerate known locally as Pudding Stone, and date from the 14th and 15th centuries. There are some good examples of medieval stained glass surviving in the windows, and a Norman font of about 1100. This rural scene is little changed today.

Binfield, Terrace Road c1955 B97005
The corner shop at the junction of Terrace Road and Forest Road displays numerous advertisements, including those for Walls Ice Cream, Cadburys, Digger, and Turf. The sign for Craven 'A' cigarettes states 'Will not affect your throat'. Further on, the local garage sells both Shell and BP petrol, and also offers car hire.

Binfield, Lodge Gates, Newbold Missionary College c1955 B97009
At the entrance to the mansion of Moor Close is the junction of Popeswood Road and St Marks Road. The lodge on the left bears a stone with the initials HHB after its original owner, and the date of the building, 1881.

Binfield, Newbold Missionary College c1955 B97008
Viewed across a new orchard is the mansion of Moore Close. The original house, built by Mr Hutchinson Brown, was bought by Charles Birch Crisp who, in 1910, commissioned newly-qualified architect Oliver Hill to enlarge the house and design the gardens. Newbold Missionary College moved to the site in February 1946.

Binfield, Salisbury Hall c1960 B97011
Completed in 1957 to increase the facilities available at Newbold College, the hall is still in use today as classrooms, church, and administration rooms. The church of the Seventh Day Adventists continues to run the college and welcomes students from across the world. The college celebrated its centenary in June 2001.

Binfield, The Stag 1892 B97001
A welcome stop for many a traveller, including the journalist William Cobbett who in 1822, recorded "at Binfield I stopped to breakfast at a very nice country inn called The Stag and Hounds". He described Forest Road, seen to the left, as "smooth as a die". Except for tarmac roads the scene has changed very little.

Around Ascot

Ascot
Grandstand 1902 48273
With the clock hands approaching 2.20pm, one can imagine the buzz of excitement as the horses raced towards the finish line. Hats were clearly the fashion of the day with not a bare head visible. The numerous policemen who appear in relaxed poses beside the railings have uninterrupted views of the passing action.

Ascot, Shepherd Whites Corner 1906 55022
The carrier has stopped, perhaps to pose, at the junction of Windsor Road and Winkfield Road. Whoever Shepherd White was, he is unlikely to have expected his name to be recorded for posterity, or to imagine 'his' junction with twin roundabouts and seemingly endless traffic as it is today.

Ascot, High Street 1903 50692
Wheel ruts are clearly visible on the unmade surface of the High Street. Sandwith & Clayton, Pharmaceutical and Dispensing Chemists, occupy the shop on the left. The group of onlookers, obviously intrigued by the camera, are standing near to the entrance of Ascot Post Office.

Ascot, High Street 1906 55013
Built by public subscription, the building on the right served as the fire station. Bearing the sign 'Ascot Fire Brigade, 1902' it is further identified by a lamp inscribed 'Fire Station'. The International Stores can be seen next door.

◀ **South Ascot High Street 1906**
55024
Here we are looking along Brockenhurst Road. In the distance we can see the line of the railway bridge and in the foreground, land on the left, as yet undeveloped. Opposite, children stand beside a shop on the corner of Spring Gardens. The shop has now been removed leaving the house to which it was joined as a private home.

◀ Ascot
High Street c1955
A64002

On the left, topped by a balustrade was the High Street Post Office. Next door are the Mascot Tea Rooms, advertising their trade in all directions. Beyond are Colebrook & Co, butchers, who also sold fish, ice and, it would appear, Hovis bread.

▼ Sunninghill
Church 1901 46887

St Michael's Church lies off the London Road at the end of Church Lane, extensively rebuilt in brick during the early 19th century. It narrowly escaped destruction on 13 September 1940 when a German bomb landed in front of the tower. Doors, windows and a small amount of masonry were damaged, but in general the church escaped remarkably intact.

◀ Sunningdale
London Road c1955 S574086

Andrews of Sunningdale can be seen on the near left. Many will remember their automaton sign of a man pushing a rotivator that advertised their garden machinery business. Further along, the store of W H Cullen occupied the shop at the junction of Chobham Road.

Crowthorne Village

Crowthorne
High Street 1925 78035
The Prince Alfred public house seen on the left was apparently
named after Queen Victoria's son, and appears much the same now
on the corner of Dukes Ride and the High Street. Just visible above
the rooftops on the right is the short spire of the Methodist Church.

Crowthorne, Church Street 1908 59486
The church of St John the Baptist, designed by Blomfield and consecrated in 1873, can be seen in the distance; the lych gate, prominent today, was not yet built. Businesses on the right included Satchells the chemist who later moved a short distance into the Sandhurst Road.

Crowthorne, High Street 1921 69933
We can see the pub sign of the Iron Duke on the left, beyond which is the gabled shop front of the International Stores, and just to its right, across Church Street, the Post Office. In the foreground on the right is Knights the chemist, having taken over from Satchells whose name was still on the shop front.

Broadmoor Asylum Entrance 1908 59488
This dominant entrance, designed by Sir Joshua Webb, is somewhat Romanesque in its style. Built in an area of open heath land and named Broadmoor Criminal Lunatic Asylum, the first admissions took place in May 1863. A variety of changes have been seen over the years. It became Broadmoor Institution after 1948, and is known today as Broadmoor Hospital.

◀ **Broadmoor Female Quarters The Asylum 1910** 62902

Just visible in the foreground is the edge of what had been a bowling green and croquet lawn, beyond which is a gravel path and the planted slope of a terrace. Two members of staff can be seen close to a covered pavilion and in the background is York House. The development of Broadmoor and, a few years earlier, Wellington College, provided the basis for Crowthorne to grow as a village, previously having been little more than an area of heath and woodland crossed by sandy roads.

**Broadmoor
Females Entrance
The Asylum 1910** 62900
Without barred windows it
would not be obvious that
this was other than a
private residence. The lush
growth of trees, shrubs and
ivy all add to the attractive
setting. The first intake of
female patients numbered
about 95.

▼ **Wellington College 1906**
57018
Designed by the architect
John Shaw, Wellington
College was opened to
pupils in January 1859. Built
as a memorial to the Duke of
Wellington, it was originally
intended to provide
schooling for the orphan
sons of British Army officers,
but in fact opened with a
mixture of both orphaned
boys and those with families.

◄ **Crowthorne
Wellington College Chapel
1906** 57021
The chapel differs in style from
the main college building, and
was designed by Gilbert Scott.
Built after the college had
opened, its foundation stone
was laid by Prince Albert in
1861 only a short time before
his death.

**Crowthorne
Wellington College
The King at
Wellington College
1909** w46301
Speech Day, the
college's Golden
Jubilee and a Royal
visit, made for a truly
special occasion.
Seated are Prince
Arthur of Connaught,
King Edward VII and
Helena Princess
Christian of Denmark.
To the rear on the left
are two unidentified
ladies, in the centre,
Queen Alexandra, and
to the right, Prince
Christian, Lord Derby,
an unidentified lady,
and the Master,
Doctor Pollock.

Crowthorne, Wellington College, The Lake Bridge 1906 57170
This is a peaceful scene, in which uniformed boys from the college are resting on the bridge. The lake is within the college grounds, which are extensive and include a number of playing fields, a large area of woodland and a variety of buildings associated with the college.

Crowthorne
Wellington College, Station Road 1908 59481
This area was within bounds for the college boys. The nearby station was then known by the name 'Wellington College Station'. Other local services included a bank, A Post Office, and a cycle dealer. The long unmade road is Dukes Ride. The building immediately on the left had been a bank prior to its demolition in the 1960s, and is now the site of a car park, with shops set back from the road. The other buildings remain, that with the large expanse of end wall is the Post Office and newsagents.

Finchampstead and Eversley

Finchampstead
Wellingtonia Avenue 1927 79647
The Avenue was opened in 1863 as a new road from Crowthorne to
Finchampstead via The Ridges, and was flanked by a total of 110 Wellingtonia
trees. It was the idea of John Walter III, owner of the vast Bearwood Estate,
who named it in commemoration of the Duke of Wellington.

Finchampstead, The Ridges 1927 79643
About 60 acres of land, known as The Ridges, were bought by public subscription in 1913 and presented to The National Trust. Set in heath land, from a viewpoint recorded as 332 feet above sea level, fine views were visible in all directions.

Finchampstead, Church 1906 57014
The parish church of St James, Finchampstead was first recorded in the early 12th century. One of its later additions was the brick tower in 1720. The church site may have been used at an earlier date and lies only a short distance from the line of The Devils Highway, a former Roman road.

▼ **Finchampstead, Church 1910** 63007
Looking towards the apse, the carved pulpit can be seen on the right.
In the foreground, the font possibly dates from the Saxon period. Oil
lamps appear to provide the only source of artificial light. Today, the
interior still conveys a magical atmosphere of great age.

▼ **Finchampstead, Village Forge c1900** F26301
We can see the farrier at work inspecting the hoof of a pony whilst his
assistant holds the bridle. It is interesting to note the enamel sign
attached to the forge wall advertising Humber Cycles. This would
suggest he was something of an entrepreneur and sought to satisfy
more than one type of customer.

▲ **Finchampstead
Post Office 1906** 57013
Living over the shop was
the order of the day as
depicted in this picture of
the village Post Office,
owned at this time by
Owen A J Goddard. The
services of a post office
continue in the village to
this day, but operate in
different premises a short
distance away.

◄ **Finchampstead**
New Mill 1908 59512
The New Mill is in fact old
and believed to date from
the 15th century. It was
powered by water from the
River Blackwater and
continued to operate until
the middle of the 20th
century. This picture was
taken near to the ford.
Much of the mill survives,
but has been converted into
a restaurant.

Finchampstead Village 1908 59513
The Post Office is just visible on the left. It appears that the horse and farrier are posing for the photograph, whilst the cart remains in front of the forge. The Monkey Puzzle tree in the garden of the thatched cottage has long since gone. It stood opposite what is now called Longwater Lane.

◀ **Eversley
Cross Green 1910** 63002
This picture shows a pond
considerably bigger than
that which remains today;
beyond lies The Lamb
public house. Today with a
reduced pond and an
enlarged green, there exists
an excellent cricket pitch, all
of which remains in full view
of the much larger pub and
restaurant now named 'Le
Toad and Stumps'.

◄ **Eversley**
Eversley Cross 1910
63006
The Inn sign of The Chequers can be seen on the left. The road sign standing on the corner of the green points left to Fleet and Hartley Wintney, right to Finchampstead and Wokingham. The cottages appear very well maintained with smart iron railings and neatly clipped hedges.

▼ **Eversley**
Eversley Cross 1910
63004
Approaching Eversley Cross from Yateley, Marsh Lane lies off to the left and the green is just visible beyond the road ahead. The fact that a watercourse passes beneath the road would easily be overlooked today, but most of the buildings remain in much the same situation.

◄ **Eversley**
Rectory, Kingsley's Study 1901 46839
Charles Kingsley (the renowned author) was the Rector of Eversley for a number of years. It was during that period he wrote his famous book 'The Water Babies', said to have been inspired by a young Wokingham chimney sweep named James Seaward, whom he portrayed as the character Tom.

Eversley Centre 1908 59508
A wagon loaded with baulks of timber is just visible heading towards Yateley and another cart is approaching on the right. The three individuals on the left are in the garden of a house that still exists and is situated to the left of the Golden Pot public house.

Eversley, The White Hart 1906 57011
The old gentleman seated in the foreground is a travelling knife grinder. His hand-cart is equipped with a grinding wheel and a can of lubricant stands on the ground beside his feet. He is seated at the roadside in front of the White Hart public house.

Yateley, The Common 1924 75556
From its depot in Reading, having stopped at Shinfield, Arborfield, Eversley and Yateley, a Thorneycroft J Type bus operated by the Thames Valley Traction Company has yet to make a pick up in Derby Green before continuing through Blackwater, to its destination in Camberley. It seems a fitting picture to conclude this selection of photographs and illustrate the pace of life in days gone by.

Index

Wokingham
All Saints Church 16, 17
Rose Street 17, 18-19
Town Hall 20, 21, 22-23, 26
Peach Street 20-21
Ye Olde Rose Inne 21
Denmark Street 22, 23
Market Place 22-23
Broad Street 24-25, 27, 28, 29
Tudor House 30
Martin's Swimming Pool 30
Reading Road 31, 33
The Queen's Head 31
The Terrace 32
Station Road 32
Public Rest Gardens 33
St Paul's Church 34, 35
Joel Park 35
Lakeside Holidays 36-37, 38-39
Kingsmere Lake 37
St Sebastian's Church 40
Nine Mile Ride 40-41
London Open Air Sanatorium 42, 43

Ascot
The Grandstand 60-612
High Street 63, 64-65
Sheperd Whites Corner 62

Binfield
Church 57
Newbold Missionary College 58
Salisbury Hall 59
The Stag 59
Terrace Road 57

Bracknell
Church Road 46-47
High Street 48-49, 50-51, 52-53
The Horse and Groom 53
Holy Trinity Church 45
Old Manor Hotel 48
The Market Inn 48
Priestwood Square 54-55

Easthampstead
Borough Green 55
Church 54, 55
Foxhills Schools 55
Point Royal 56

Eversley
Cross Green 82
Eversley Cross 82-83
The Rectory 83
The White Hart 86
Village Centre 85

Finchampstead
Church 77, 78
New Mill 79
Post Office 78-79, 80-81
The Ridges 77
Village Forge 78
Wellingtonia Avenue 76

Surrounding Area
Broadmoor Asylum 68-69, 70-71
Crowthorne 66, 67
Sunningdale 65
Sunninghill 65
Warfield 44
Wellington College 71, 72-73, 74, 75
Yately 86

Frith Book Co Titles

www.francisfrith.co.uk

The Frith Book Company publishes over 100 new titles each year. A selection of those currently available are listed below. For latest catalogue please contact Frith Book Co.

Town Books 96 pages, approx 100 photos. County and Themed Books 128 pages, approx 150 photos (unless specified). All titles hardback laminated case and jacket except those indicated pb (paperback)

Amersham, Chesham & Rickmansworth (pb)			Derby (pb)	1-85937-367-4	£9.99
	1-85937-340-2	£9.99	Derbyshire (pb)	1-85937-196-5	£9.99
Ancient Monuments & Stone Circles	1-85937-143-4	£17.99	Devon (pb)	1-85937-297-x	£9.99
Aylesbury (pb)	1-85937-227-9	£9.99	Dorset (pb)	1-85937-269-4	£9.99
Bakewell	1-85937-113-2	£12.99	Dorset Churches	1-85937-172-8	£17.99
Barnstaple (pb)	1-85937-300-3	£9.99	Dorset Coast (pb)	1-85937-299-6	£9.99
Bath (pb)	1-85937419-0	£9.99	Dorset Living Memories	1-85937-210-4	£14.99
Bedford (pb)	1-85937-205-8	£9.99	Down the Severn	1-85937-118-3	£14.99
Berkshire (pb)	1-85937-191-4	£9.99	Down the Thames (pb)	1-85937-278-3	£9.99
Berkshire Churches	1-85937-170-1	£17.99	Down the Trent	1-85937-311-9	£14.99
Blackpool (pb)	1-85937-382-8	£9.99	Dublin (pb)	1-85937-231-7	£9.99
Bognor Regis (pb)	1-85937-431-x	£9.99	East Anglia (pb)	1-85937-265-1	£9.99
Bournemouth	1-85937-067-5	£12.99	East London	1-85937-080-2	£14.99
Bradford (pb)	1-85937-204-x	£9.99	East Sussex	1-85937-130-2	£14.99
Brighton & Hove(pb)	1-85937-192-2	£8.99	Eastbourne	1-85937-061-6	£12.99
Bristol (pb)	1-85937-264-3	£9.99	Edinburgh (pb)	1-85937-193-0	£8.99
British Life A Century Ago (pb)	1-85937-213-9	£9.99	England in the 1880s	1-85937-331-3	£17.99
Buckinghamshire (pb)	1-85937-200-7	£9.99	English Castles (pb)	1-85937-434-4	£9.99
Camberley (pb)	1-85937-222-8	£9.99	English Country Houses	1-85937-161-2	£17.99
Cambridge (pb)	1-85937-422-0	£9.99	Essex (pb)	1-85937-270-8	£9.99
Cambridgeshire (pb)	1-85937-420-4	£9.99	Exeter	1-85937-126-4	£12.99
Canals & Waterways (pb)	1-85937-291-0	£9.99	Exmoor	1-85937-132-9	£14.99
Canterbury Cathedral (pb)	1-85937-179-5	£9.99	Falmouth	1-85937-066-7	£12.99
Cardiff (pb)	1-85937-093-4	£9.99	Folkestone (pb)	1-85937-124-8	£9.99
Carmarthenshire	1-85937-216-3	£14.99	Glasgow (pb)	1-85937-190-6	£9.99
Chelmsford (pb)	1-85937-310-0	£9.99	Gloucestershire	1-85937-102-7	£14.99
Cheltenham (pb)	1-85937-095-0	£9.99	Great Yarmouth (pb)	1-85937-426-3	£9.99
Cheshire (pb)	1-85937-271-6	£9.99	Greater Manchester (pb)	1-85937-266-x	£9.99
Chester	1-85937-090-x	£12.99	Guildford (pb)	1-85937-410-7	£9.99
Chesterfield	1-85937-378-x	£9.99	Hampshire (pb)	1-85937-279-1	£9.99
Chichester (pb)	1-85937-228-7	£9.99	Hampshire Churches (pb)	1-85937-207-4	£9.99
Colchester (pb)	1-85937-188-4	£8.99	Harrogate	1-85937-423-9	£9.99
Cornish Coast	1-85937-163-9	£14.99	Hastings & Bexhill (pb)	1-85937-131-0	£9.99
Cornwall (pb)	1-85937-229-5	£9.99	Heart of Lancashire (pb)	1-85937-197-3	£9.99
Cornwall Living Memories	1-85937-248-1	£14.99	Helston (pb)	1-85937-214-7	£9.99
Cotswolds (pb)	1-85937-230-9	£9.99	Hereford (pb)	1-85937-175-2	£9.99
Cotswolds Living Memories	1-85937-255-4	£14.99	Herefordshire	1-85937-174-4	£14.99
County Durham	1-85937-123-x	£14.99	Hertfordshire (pb)	1-85937-247-3	£9.99
Croydon Living Memories	1-85937-162-0	£9.99	Horsham (pb)	1-85937-432-8	£9.99
Cumbria	1-85937-101-9	£14.99	Humberside	1-85937-215-5	£14.99
Dartmoor	1-85937-145-0	£14.99	Hythe, Romney Marsh & Ashford	1-85937-256-2	£9.99

Available from your local bookshop or from the publisher

Frith Book Co Titles (continued)

Title	ISBN	Price
Ipswich (pb)	1-85937-424-7	£9.99
Ireland (pb)	1-85937-181-7	£9.99
Isle of Man (pb)	1-85937-268-6	£9.99
Isles of Scilly	1-85937-136-1	£14.99
Isle of Wight (pb)	1-85937-429-8	£9.99
Isle of Wight Living Memories	1-85937-304-6	£14.99
Kent (pb)	1-85937-189-2	£9.99
Kent Living Memories	1-85937-125-6	£14.99
Lake District (pb)	1-85937-275-9	£9.99
Lancaster, Morecambe & Heysham (pb)	1-85937-233-3	£9.99
Leeds (pb)	1-85937-202-3	£9.99
Leicester	1-85937-073-x	£12.99
Leicestershire (pb)	1-85937-185-x	£9.99
Lincolnshire (pb)	1-85937-433-6	£9.99
Liverpool & Merseyside (pb)	1-85937-234-1	£9.99
London (pb)	1-85937-183-3	£9.99
Ludlow (pb)	1-85937-176-0	£9.99
Luton (pb)	1-85937-235-x	£9.99
Maidstone	1-85937-056-x	£14.99
Manchester (pb)	1-85937-198-1	£9.99
Middlesex	1-85937-158-2	£14.99
New Forest	1-85937-128-0	£14.99
Newark (pb)	1-85937-366-6	£9.99
Newport, Wales (pb)	1-85937-258-9	£9.99
Newquay (pb)	1-85937-421-2	£9.99
Norfolk (pb)	1-85937-195-7	£9.99
Norfolk Living Memories	1-85937-217-1	£14.99
Northamptonshire	1-85937-150-7	£14.99
Northumberland Tyne & Wear (pb)	1-85937-281-3	£9.99
North Devon Coast	1-85937-146-9	£14.99
North Devon Living Memories	1-85937-261-9	£14.99
North London	1-85937-206-6	£14.99
North Wales (pb)	1-85937-298-8	£9.99
North Yorkshire (pb)	1-85937-236-8	£9.99
Norwich (pb)	1-85937-194-9	£8.99
Nottingham (pb)	1-85937-324-0	£9.99
Nottinghamshire (pb)	1-85937-187-6	£9.99
Oxford (pb)	1-85937-411-5	£9.99
Oxfordshire (pb)	1-85937-430-1	£9.99
Peak District (pb)	1-85937-280-5	£9.99
Penzance	1-85937-069-1	£12.99
Peterborough (pb)	1-85937-219-8	£9.99
Piers	1-85937-237-6	£17.99
Plymouth	1-85937-119-1	£12.99
Poole & Sandbanks (pb)	1-85937-251-1	£9.99
Preston (pb)	1-85937-212-0	£9.99
Reading (pb)	1-85937-238-4	£9.99
Romford (pb)	1-85937-319-4	£9.99
Salisbury (pb)	1-85937-239-2	£9.99
Scarborough (pb)	1-85937-379-8	£9.99
St Albans (pb)	1-85937-341-0	£9.99
St Ives (pb)	1-85937415-8	£9.99
Scotland (pb)	1-85937-182-5	£9.99
Scottish Castles (pb)	1-85937-323-2	£9.99
Sevenoaks & Tunbridge	1-85937-057-8	£12.99
Sheffield, South Yorks (pb)	1-85937-267-8	£9.99
Shrewsbury (pb)	1-85937-325-9	£9.99
Shropshire (pb)	1-85937-326-7	£9.99
Somerset	1-85937-153-1	£14.99
South Devon Coast	1-85937-107-8	£14.99
South Devon Living Memories	1-85937-168-x	£14.99
South Hams	1-85937-220-1	£14.99
Southampton (pb)	1-85937-427-1	£9.99
Southport (pb)	1-85937-425-5	£9.99
Staffordshire	1-85937-047-0	£12.99
Stratford upon Avon	1-85937-098-5	£12.99
Suffolk (pb)	1-85937-221-x	£9.99
Suffolk Coast	1-85937-259-7	£14.99
Surrey (pb)	1-85937-240-6	£9.99
Sussex (pb)	1-85937-184-1	£9.99
Swansea (pb)	1-85937-167-1	£9.99
Tees Valley & Cleveland	1-85937-211-2	£14.99
Thanet (pb)	1-85937-116-7	£9.99
Tiverton (pb)	1-85937-178-7	£9.99
Torbay	1-85937-063-2	£12.99
Truro	1-85937-147-7	£12.99
Victorian and Edwardian Cornwall	1-85937-252-x	£14.99
Victorian & Edwardian Devon	1-85937-253-8	£14.99
Victorian & Edwardian Kent	1-85937-149-3	£14.99
Vic & Ed Maritime Album	1-85937-144-2	£17.99
Victorian and Edwardian Sussex	1-85937-157-4	£14.99
Victorian & Edwardian Yorkshire	1-85937-154-x	£14.99
Victorian Seaside	1-85937-159-0	£17.99
Villages of Devon (pb)	1-85937-293-7	£9.99
Villages of Kent (pb)	1-85937-294-5	£9.99
Villages of Sussex (pb)	1-85937-295-3	£9.99
Warwickshire (pb)	1-85937-203-1	£9.99
Welsh Castles (pb)	1-85937-322-4	£9.99
West Midlands (pb)	1-85937-289-9	£9.99
West Sussex	1-85937-148-5	£14.99
West Yorkshire (pb)	1-85937-201-5	£9.99
Weymouth (pb)	1-85937-209-0	£9.99
Wiltshire (pb)	1-85937-277-5	£9.99
Wiltshire Churches (pb)	1-85937-171-x	£9.99
Wiltshire Living Memories	1-85937-245-7	£14.99
Winchester (pb)	1-85937-428-x	£9.99
Windmills & Watermills	1-85937-242-2	£17.99
Worcester (pb)	1-85937-165-5	£9.99
Worcestershire	1-85937-152-3	£14.99
York (pb)	1-85937-199-x	£9.99
Yorkshire (pb)	1-85937-186-8	£9.99
Yorkshire Living Memories	1-85937-166-3	£14.99

See Frith books on the internet www.francisfrith.co.uk

FRITH PRODUCTS & SERVICES

Francis Frith would doubtless be pleased to know that the pioneering publishing venture he started in 1860 still continues today. Over a hundred and forty years later, The Francis Frith Collection continues in the same innovative tradition and is now one of the foremost publishers of vintage photographs in the world. Some of the current activities include:

Interior Decoration

Today Frith's photographs can be seen framed and as giant wall murals in thousands of pubs, restaurants, hotels, banks, retail stores and other public buildings throughout the country. In every case they enhance the unique local atmosphere of the places they depict and provide reminders of gentler days in an increasingly busy and frenetic world.

Product Promotions

Frith products are used by many major companies to promote the sales of their own products or to reinforce their own history and heritage. Frith promotions have been used by Hovis bread, Courage beers, Scots Porage Oats, Colman's mustard, Cadbury's foods, Mellow Birds coffee, Dunhill pipe tobacco, Guinness, and Bulmer's Cider.

Genealogy and Family History

As the interest in family history and roots grows world-wide, more and more people are turning to Frith's photographs of Great Britain for images of the towns, villages and streets where their ancestors lived; and, of course, photographs of the churches and chapels where their ancestors were christened, married and buried are an essential part of every genealogy tree and family album.

Frith Products

All Frith photographs are available Framed or just as Mounted Prints and Posters (size 23 x 16 inches). These may be ordered from the address below. From time to time other products - Address Books, Calendars, Table Mats, etc - are available.

The Internet

Already fifty thousand Frith photographs can be viewed and purchased on the internet through the Frith websites and a myriad of partner sites.

For more detailed information on Frith companies and products, look at these sites:

www.francisfrith.co.uk
www.francisfrith.com
(for North American visitors)

See the complete list of Frith Books at:

www.francisfrith.co.uk

This web site is regularly updated with the latest list of publications from the Frith Book Company. If you wish to buy books relating to another part of the country that your local bookshop does not stock, you may purchase on-line.

For further information, trade, or author enquiries please contact us at the address below:
The Francis Frith Collection, Frith's Barn, Teffont, Salisbury, Wiltshire, England SP3 5QP.
Tel: +44 (0)1722 716 376 Fax: +44 (0)1722 716 881 Email: sales@francisfrith.co.uk

See Frith books on the internet at www.francisfrith.co.uk

FREE MOUNTED PRINT

Mounted Print
Overall size 14 x 11 inches

Fill in and cut out this voucher and return
it with your remittance for £2.25 (to cover postage and handling). Offer valid for delivery to UK addresses only.

Choose any photograph included in this book.
Your SEPIA print will be A4 in size. It will be mounted in a cream mount with a burgundy rule line (overall size 14 x 11 inches).

**Order additional Mounted Prints
at HALF PRICE (only £7.49 each*)**
If you would like to order more Frith prints from this book, possibly as gifts for friends and family, you can buy them at half price (with no additional postage and handling costs).

Have your Mounted Prints framed
For an extra £14.95 per print* you can have your mounted print(s) framed in an elegant polished wood and gilt moulding, overall size 16 x 13 inches (no additional postage and handling required).

---

* IMPORTANT!

These special prices are only available if you order at the same time as you order your free mounted print. You must use the ORIGINAL VOUCHER on this page (no copies permitted). We can only despatch to one address.

Send completed Voucher form to:
The Francis Frith Collection, Frith's Barn, Teffont, Salisbury, Wiltshire SP3 5QP

CHOOSE ANY IMAGE FROM THIS BOOK

Voucher for **FREE** *and Reduced Price Frith Prints*

Please do not photocopy this voucher. Only the original is valid, so please fill it in, cut it out and return it to us with your order.

Picture ref no	Page no	Qty	Mounted @ £7.49	Framed + £14.95	Total Cost
		1	Free of charge*	£	£
			£7.49	£	£
			£7.49	£	£
			£7.49	£	£
			£7.49	£	£
			£7.49	£	£
Please allow 28 days for delivery			* Post & handling (UK)		£2.25
			Total Order Cost		£

Title of this book . . . .

I enclose a cheque/postal order for £ . . . .
made payable to 'The Francis Frith Collection'

OR please debit my Mastercard / Visa / Switch / Amex card
(credit cards please on all overseas orders), details below

Card Number

Issue No (Switch only)   Valid from (Amex/Switch)

Expires   Signature

Name Mr/Mrs/Ms . . . .

Address . . . .

. . . .

. . . .

. . . . Postcode . . . .

Daytime Tel No . . . .

Email . . . .

Valid to 31/12/05

Would you like to find out more about Francis Frith?

We have recently recruited some entertaining speakers who are happy to visit local groups, clubs and societies to give an illustrated talk documenting Frith's travels and photographs. If you are a member of such a group and are interested in hosting a presentation, we would love to hear from you.

Our speakers bring with them a small selection of our local town and county books, together with sample prints. They are happy to take orders. A small proportion of the order value is donated to the group who have hosted the presentation. The talks are therefore an excellent way of fundraising for small groups and societies.

Can you help us with information about any of the Frith photographs in this book?

We are gradually compiling an historical record for each of the photographs in the Frith archive. It is always fascinating to find out the names of the people shown in the pictures, as well as insights into the shops, buildings and other features depicted.

If you recognize anyone in the photographs in this book, or if you have information not already included in the author's caption, do let us know. We would love to hear from you, and will try to publish it in future books or articles.

Our production team

Frith books are produced by a small dedicated team at offices in the converted Grade II listed 18th-century barn at Teffont near Salisbury, illustrated above. Most have worked with the Frith Collection for many years. All have in common one quality: they have a passion for the Frith Collection. The team is constantly expanding, but currently includes:

Jason Buck, John Buck, Douglas Mitchell-Burns, Ruth Butler, Heather Crisp, Isobel Hall, Julian Hight, Peter Horne, James Kinnear, Karen Kinnear, Tina Leary, David Marsh, Sue Molloy, Kate Rotondetto, Dean Scource, Eliza Sackett, Terence Sackett, Sandra Sampson, Adrian Sanders, Sandra Sanger, Julia Skinner, Lewis Taylor, Shelley Tolcher and Lorraine Tuck.